NATURE UNLEASHED

TSUNAMIS

Louise and Richard Spilsbury

W
FRANKLIN WATTS
LONDON·SYDNEY

Franklin Watts
First published in Great Britain in 2016 by The Watts Publishing Group

Credits
Series Editors: Sarah Eason and Harriet McGregor
Series Designer: Simon Borrough
Picture Researcher: Rachel Blount

Picture credits: Cover: Shutterstock: M Taira; Inside: NOAA/National Geophysical Data
Center: Cpl. Megan Angel, U.S. Marine Corps 25, Hugh Davies. University of PNG 17,
Katherine Mueller, IFRC 1, Harry Yeh, University of Washington 9l, 9r; Shutterstock:
3777190317 27, Anton Balazh 19, Steven Collins 4–5, Johan W. Elzenga 6–7, Everett
Historical 13, Nickolay Stanev 21, Wickerwood 7; USGS: 11, 23; Wikimedia Commons:
Nesnad/The Osaka Mainichi 15.

Every attempt has been made to clear copyright. Should there be any inadvertent
omission please apply to the publisher for rectification.

HB ISBN: 978 1 4451 5393 3

Printed in China

Franklin Watts
An imprint of
Hachette Children's Group
Part of The Watts Publishing Group
Carmelite House
50 Victoria Embankment
London EC4Y 0DZ

An Hachette UK Company
www.hachette.co.uk

www.franklinwatts.co.uk

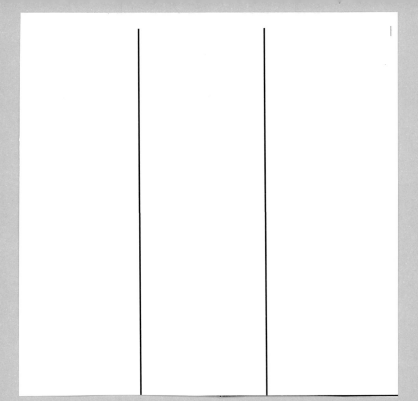

Contents

TSUNAMI DANGER

Tsunamis are huge and destructive ocean waves that can cause terrible devastation. A tsunami may hit land as a high and fast-moving wall of water, destroying or sweeping away everything in its path.

This valley in Thailand was completely **engulfed** during a tsunami.

How Dangerous?

Smaller tsunamis may arrive on a coastline like a quickly rising **tide**. They might only gently flood towns right by the seashore. Other tsunamis are vast. These waves can be 40 metres (m) above the normal level of the sea. They can crash onto land with the same force as a wall of concrete. They **submerge** people, animals, buildings and farms. They can carry boats, vehicles and parts of buildings many kilometres inland. Entire coastlines can be altered by a tsunami.

Measuring Disaster

Scientists are working on systems that will give a warning when a tsunami is about to happen.

Most tsunamis are caused by **earthquakes** at the bottom of the ocean.

→

Seismologists use **seismometers** to record when and where earthquakes happen and how strong they are.

When a tsunami begins, there is a sudden change in **sea level**.

→

Scientists have **sensors** in the oceans that can detect a deep tsunami wave passing over them.

Tsunamis cause more damage on areas of flat land at the coast.

→

Scientists make computer models of coastal areas to see how far tsunamis would travel inland. They then know which communities to **evacuate**.

Natural disasters have taken place since the Earth was formed. People have many ways of deciding what the world's worst natural disasters have been, from the deadliest disaster to the costliest. This book includes some of the worst tsunami disasters in history.

TSUNAMIS IN ACTION

Tsunamis usually happen when an earthquake makes the ground shake at the bottom of the ocean. This moves millions of tonnes of seawater and creates a series of waves on the ocean's surface. These waves can become tsunamis.

Tsunami Forces

The Earth's outer layer, or **crust**, is made up of giant plates of rock. These huge, gigantic slabs fit together like a jigsaw puzzle. They are called **tectonic plates**. The plates are always moving slightly because they sit on a layer of hot, melted rock deep inside the Earth.

As the plates move, they push and slide against each other. When one sticks and then suddenly slips, seawater rushes in to fill the gap. This sudden movement in the ocean causes giant waves, or tsunamis. These tsunamis travel quickly over long distances through deep water. As they near land, the waves slow down and pile up. They can build to great heights by the time they reach the coast.

A fishing boat washed up high on shore by the force of a tsunami.

Volcanoes and Landslides

Some tsunamis happen when an underwater **volcano** explodes. Volcanoes expel hot liquid rock from beneath the crust when they erupt. This dislodges rocks around the volcano, causing large movements of water, which in turn may start a tsunami.

Other tsunamis happen when **landslides** send large amounts of rock or ice down into the water. In 1958 in Lituya Bay, Alaska, a landslide dumped 81.6 million tonnes of rock into the bay. The result was a tsunami that reached 525 m up the slope on the other side of the bay.

Tsunami waves are at their tallest when they reach the seashore. They can still be moving at hundreds of kilometres per hour (kph).

10 FLORES SEA

A large earthquake occurred just off the north coast of Flores Island, Indonesia, early in the morning of 12 December 1992. It set off a series of devastating tsunamis, which arrived on the shores of Flores within 5 minutes.

Flores Sea

INDONESIA

Babi Island

Flores Island

A Lost Island

The tsunami hit and caused massive damage on both Flores and Babi Island. Babi Island is a volcanic island between Flores Island and the earthquake **epicentre** in the Flores Sea. On Babi Island, the tsunami hit a narrow stretch of flat land on which two villages were located. The wave rose 7 m above sea level, swept away all of the wooden homes and killed 263 people. A few survivors swam 5 kilometres (km) to Flores Island, where they told stories of bodies left dangling in trees after the disaster.

On the Record

The tsunami carried water almost 300 m inland. Wave heights of more than 25 m were reported on Flores Island.

The death toll from both the earthquake and tsunami was more than 2,000. The tsunami caused about half of those deaths.

The tsunami flattened trees and approximately 18,000 houses along the coast.

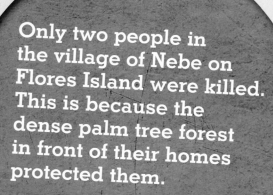

Only two people in the village of Nebe on Flores Island were killed. This is because the dense palm tree forest in front of their homes protected them.

A long, heavily populated **peninsula** off Flores was flooded by water that destroyed 80 per cent of the area's wooden stilt houses and killed 87 people.

9 PACIFIC OCEAN

The tsunami that hit Chile on 22 May 1960 was caused by the largest earthquake recorded in the twentieth century. The earthquake itself was massive, but most of the injuries and deaths were caused by the tsunami that followed it, just 15 minutes later.

Los Angeles

San Diego

JAPAN

UNITED STATES

Hawaii

Far-Reaching Waves

The tsunami waves rose up to 25 m high on parts of the Chilean coastline. They wiped out entire areas and at least 200 people died in Chile alone. The shifts in the ocean floor caused by the quake were so enormous that the tsunami reached as far as Hawaii and Japan, thousands of kilometres away, where they caused more destruction. In Japan, the tsunami destroyed 1,600 homes and killed nearly 200 people.

Chile

On the Record

Tsunami waves travelled 10,000 km and hit Hawaii nearly 15 hours after the earthquake.

In Hawaii, 11-m-high waves caused millions of pounds of damage in Hilo Bay, killing 61 people.

When the waves reached Japan, 22 hours after the quake, the waves were still 5.5 m high.

In Japan, the tsunami was still strong enough to cause terrible damage and smash these ships into a bridge.

In Chile, the waves carried the remains of people's homes up to 3.2 km inland.

Waves that approached California on the Pacific Coast of the United States were up to 1.7 m high. They damaged boats and **docks** in Los Angeles, San Diego and Long Beach.

8 NANKAIDŌ

Japan experiences about 1,500 earthquakes every year, mostly small, because the country sits above four tectonic plates. In 1946, the largest earthquake ever recorded in Japan shook the seabed off the coast of Honshu, Japan's main island. It was a massive 8.1 magnitude quake and caused three major tsunamis.

Honshu   JAPAN

Kyushu

Nankaidō

Striking the Coast

The enormous quake and tsunamis inflicted terrible damage on the people and homes along the coast of Nankaidō region in south-west Japan. The quake happened on the evening of 20 December and shook most of Japan, from the largest, central island, Honshu, down to Kyushu. The worst loss of life happened within an hour when the tsunamis hit the coast.

On the Record

Three tsunamis struck at 20-minute intervals. The middle one was the worst, with waves up to 6 m high.

Japan was in turmoil in 1946 after the end of the Second World War. It had heavy bomb damage, widespread hunger and homelessness. The earthquake and tsunamis made a bad situation worse.

Even before the earthquake, many people were homeless, such as these men sleeping on the steps of a Tokyo subway station.

The tsunamis completely washed away over 2,000 homes and destroyed tens of thousands more.

The worst damage happened on the Kii Peninsula, which was the land closest to the offshore epicentre.

About 1,362 people were killed by the tsunamis.

7 TOKYO-YOKOHAMA

Japan is hit by a tsunami at least once a year. The tsunami that occurred at noon on 1 September 1923 was set off by a huge undersea earthquake 96 km south of Tokyo, Japan's capital city. The quake shook the ground for more than 4 minutes.

JAPAN

Atami

Tokyo-Yokohama

A Day of Terror

The earthquake caused tectonic plates around Sagami Bay to lift up by 2 m and to move horizontally by up to 4.5 m. This rupture of the ocean floor generated a tsunami that reached heights of over 6 m, flooding many low-lying areas along the coast. The quake, landslides and tsunami, as well as huge fires started by cooking stoves, destroyed much of Tokyo and nearby Yokohama.

On the Record

A series of huge waves swept away thousands of people in Yokohama, the biggest port city in Japan.

The earthquake, tsunami, fires and landslides killed 140,000 people.

The tsunami waves reached heights of 12 m at Atami, on the Sagami **Gulf**, destroying 155 homes and killing 60 people.

Each year on 1 September there is a national Disaster Prevention Day in Japan.

This image shows what was left of the Asakusa district of Tokyo after the disaster.

6 PAPUA NEW GUINEA

Imagine a quiet fishing village in the early evening as it is growing dark. Suddenly, they feel an earthquake strike and the villages are thrown into chaos and terror as huge tsunami waves roll in. This is what happened in Papua New Guinea on 17 July 1998.

Papua New Guinea

Aitape

Chaos

The epicentre of the quake was only 19 km off the coast of Papua New Guinea. Within minutes it created three large tsunami waves that battered the region. When the waves hit the 30-km stretch of beach west of the town of Aitape, most people were in their homes. They had been given no warning the quake and tsunami might happen. The tsunami killed over 2,000 people and left many more homeless.

On the Record

The largest of the tsunami waves were 10 m high.

This school building was carried 65 m by the tsunami until it was caught in palm trees.

Most of the deaths occurred in two villages on a narrow **spit** of land that separates the Sissano **Lagoon** from the ocean. Each village had about 1,800–2,000 inhabitants. All of the villagers' homes were swept away.

The tsunami ripped palm trees out of the ground.

Paul Saroya, a survivor who lost eight members of his family, commented: 'We just saw the sea rise up and it came toward the village and we had to run for our lives.'

After the first three giant waves, there was a short rest before a final, less powerful wave hit. Within 20 minutes of the quake, the ocean was quiet again.

5 SANRIKU

A powerful earthquake occurred on 2 March 1933 in the Sanriku region of Japan and caused a terrible tsunami. Waves higher than six double-decker buses stacked on top of one another rolled in across the region.

Sanriku

Honshu

JAPAN

Hawaii

Mighty Waves

The earthquake had a magnitude of 8.4 but it did little damage to buildings along the coast as most of the damage was caused by the tsunami. This is because the earthquake occurred about 290 km off the coast of Japan. The shaking of the ground was less severe by the time it reached dry land. The large tsunami hit the coast 30 minutes after the quake. More than 3,000 people lost their lives.

On the Record

About 5,000 houses in Japan were destroyed, of which nearly 3,000 were washed away.

At Ryori Bay, Honshu, waves 29 m high led to many deaths and terrible damage to homes and other buildings.

This is the Sanriku region hit by the tsunami in 1933.

• Taro
• Ryori Bay

At the town of Taro, the waves reached a height of 10 m, destroying 98 per cent of the homes and killing almost half of its inhabitants.

The tsunami also caused slight damage in Hawaii, thousands of kilometres away, where a 2.9-m-high wave was recorded on the coast of the main island.

4 ANDAMAN SEA

Most of the earthquakes that happen in the Andaman Sea, even larger-magnitude earthquakes, do not usually cause big tsunamis. The earthquake that struck near the Andaman and Nicobar Islands of India on 26 June 1941 was one of the biggest exceptions to this rule.

Andaman Sea

INDIA

Chennai ●

SRI LANKA   Bay of Bengal

Andaman and Nicobar Islands ●

Tsunami Destruction

This major earthquake happened just before noon around 20 km west of Middle Andaman Island. The jolt in the seafloor caused a tsunami in the Andaman Sea and the Bay of Bengal. The wave hit India's east coast and Sri Lanka. It killed about 5,000 people on the hundreds of islands making up the Andaman and Nicobar Islands and along the east coast of India.

On the Record

The earthquake struck with a magnitude of 8.1. It caused buildings to shake in Madras (now Chennai), in India, over 1,300 km away.

Some newspaper accounts from the time suggest that the tsunami may have been more than 1.25 m high. This would have submerged many low-lying parts of the region.

The low lying Andaman and Nicobar Islands are the peaks of a submerged mountain range and are at high risk of being flooded by tsunamis.

The Moken people, a tribe of **sea nomads** in the area, have legends about the sea being sucked away before giant waves come, which is what happens in a tsunami. It is possible that some escaped to higher ground as soon as they saw the sea retreat.

The earthquake was caused by northwards movement of part of the Earth's crust. Over millions of years, this movement formed the Himalayas and Everest, the world's tallest mountain.

3 MORO GULF

The Moro Gulf is the largest gulf in the Philippines. It is located off the coast of Mindanao Island and is part of the Celebes Sea. A few minutes after midnight on 17 August 1976, while most people were sleeping, a powerful earthquake struck the region.

PHILIPPINES

Mindanao Island
● Lebak
Celebes Sea

Moro Gulf

Midnight Killer

People had no idea what was about to hit them that night. Less than 5 minutes after the earthquake, huge tsunami waves reached the shore and swept through villages along the Moro Gulf, affecting 700 km of coastline. Official counts put the death toll for the earthquake and tsunami at more than 8,000, including those missing and never found. It is believed that the tsunami was responsible for 85 per cent of those deaths.

On the Record

The 1976 tsunami was the most destructive ever to hit the Philippines.

Some of the tsunami waves reached heights of up to 9 m.

The tsunami left over 90,000 people homeless.

Tsunami damage was widespread at Lebak on Mindanao Island in the Moro Gulf.

In some places, the tsunami waves roared 500 m inland, washing away hundreds of homes.

Eyewitnesses said the tsunami made houses rock like boats caught in a storm and sounded like the rumbling of many lorries.

2 TŌHŌKU

At 2.46 p.m. on 11 March 2011 a powerful undersea earthquake off the north-eastern coast of Japan caused widespread damage on land. It also created a series of large tsunami waves. These crashed down on many coastal areas, especially in the Tōhōku region, and caused a major accident at a nuclear power station along the coast.

Aleutian Islands

UNITED STATES

JAPAN • Oshima Tōhōku
Fukushima

Hawaii

A Powerful Tsunami

As well as hitting the coast of Japan, tsunami waves moved at speeds of up to 800 kilometres per hour (kph) in the opposite direction. They swept up to 3.6 m high along the coasts of two islands in Hawaii and caused waves 1.5 m high along one of the Aleutian Islands, 3,950 km away. Hours later, tsunami waves were still 2.7 m high when they struck the coast of the United States. The effect of the tsunami continues to be felt years after it hit Japan — many people in the worst-hit areas, such as Tōhōku, have had to move to other parts of the country.

On the Record

Most of the 19,300 deaths were caused by the tsunami waves.

One wave measured 10 m high; another swept 10 km inland.

At Uranohama Port, Oshima, these two ferries were found on the road leading to the harbour still attached to their concrete pier.

As the water from the tsunami washed back into the sea, it carried people and huge amounts of **debris** with it. Large stretches of land were also left underwater.

Tsunami waves wrecked the Fukushima nuclear plant. More than 60,000 people were evacuated from the surrounding area and high **radiation** levels mean that most have never been able to return home.

1 INDIAN OCEAN

Locals and tourists in countries around the Indian Ocean were going about their daily lives on 26 December 2004 when a huge undersea earthquake hit. It happened off the coast of the Indonesian island of Sumatra and set off a massive tsunami. A series of gigantic waves caused widespread destruction and killed a staggering number of people.

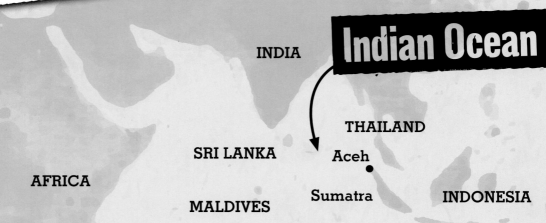

INDIA

Indian Ocean

THAILAND

SRI LANKA

Aceh

AFRICA

Sumatra

INDONESIA

MALDIVES

Worst Tsunami

The earthquake struck at 8.00 a.m. Within 2 hours, tsunami waves hit the eastern coasts of India and Sri Lanka, about 1,200 km away. Five hours after that, tsunami waves hit the coast of East Africa, more than 3,000 km away. The tsunami killed people in 12 countries, with Indonesia, Sri Lanka, India, the Maldives and Thailand suffering the worst damage. Many people suffered terrible trauma as a result of the disaster. To this day, some have never recovered the bodies of family members and loved ones.

On the Record

The tsunami killed more than 225,000 people across the globe.

In the open ocean, the tsunami was less than one metre high. When it made landfall, its height increased to 15 m in some places.

The tsunami travelled at speeds of up to 800 kph.

Aceh, in Indonesia, was devastated by the 2004 tsunami.

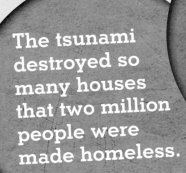

The tsunami destroyed so many houses that two million people were made homeless.

Since the disaster, the countries surrounding the Indian Ocean have set up a joint early-warning system.

A survivor described being caught in the tsunami water full of debris as, '... like being in a giant washing machine full of nails on a spin cycle.'

WHERE IN THE WORLD?

This map shows the locations of the tsunamis featured in this book.

ATLANTIC OCEAN

Read the case studies about the tsunami in the Indian Ocean in 2004, the number one tsunami in this book, and the tsunami in the Flores Sea in 1992, which is number 10. How are they similar and how do they differ?

Describe in your own words some of the ways in which people can monitor tsunamis and give people enough warning to escape.

PACIFIC OCEAN

Chile

28

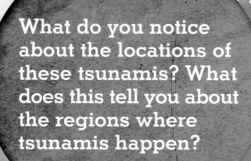

What do you notice about the locations of these tsunamis? What does this tell you about the regions where tsunamis happen?

Sanriku

Tōhōku

Tokyo–Yokohama

Nankaidō

PACIFIC OCEAN

Moro Gulf

Andaman Sea

Indian Ocean

Papua New Guinea

Flores Sea

INDIAN OCEAN

GLOSSARY

crust the Earth's outer layer of solid rock

debris loose waste material

docks partly enclosed areas in ports for ships to load and unload

earthquakes sudden violent shaking of the ground

engulfed swept over and covered

epicentre point on the Earth's surface above the place where an earthquake started

evacuate get away from an area that is dangerous to somewhere that is safe

gulf a deep inlet of the ocean or sea, almost surrounded by land, with a narrow entrance

lagoon a stretch of salt water separated from the ocean or sea by a low sandbank or coral reef

landslides collapses of masses of earth or rock from mountains or cliffs

magnitude size, particularly of an earthquake, where 1 is small and 10 is the biggest

peninsula a finger of land projecting out into a body of water

radiation a type of strong, dangerous energy produced by nuclear reactions

sea level the average height of the ocean's surface

sea nomads people who move from place to place in boats, setting up temporary camps on shore

seismologists scientists who study earthquakes

seismometers machines that measure the movement of the ground during a volcano or earthquake

sensors devices that detect and measure something such as wave height

spit a narrow coastal land formation that is linked to the coast at one end

submerge completely cover with water

tectonic plates the giant pieces of rock that fit together like a jigsaw puzzle to form the Earth's crust

tide the regular rise or fall of the ocean water at the coast

volcano an opening in the Earth's crust from which melted rock and hot gases erupt, often forming a cone-shaped mountain

FURTHER READING

Books

Surviving Tsunamis (Children's True Stories),
Kevin Cunningham, Raintree

Tsunami Disasters (Catastrophe!), John Hawkins,
Franklin Watts

Tsunami Surges (Planet in Peril), Cath Senker, Wayland

Websites

Watch this short video for an explanation of how tectonic plates
move and produce tsunamis:
**www.bbc.co.uk/science/earth/natural_disasters/
tsunami#p00fnhvm**

Discover 15 fun facts about tsunamis at:
www.fun-facts.org.uk/earth/tsunami.htm

Find out what causes tsunamis, how fast they move and other
fascinating facts at:
www.ngkids.co.uk/science-and-nature/tsunamis

Note to parents and teachers
Every effort has been made by the Publisher to ensure that
these websites contain no inappropriate or offensive material.
However, because of the nature of the Internet, it is impossible
to guarantee that the contents of these sites will not be altered.
We strongly advise that Internet access is supervised by a
responsible adult.

INDEX

These are the lists of contents for each title in *Nature Unleashed:*

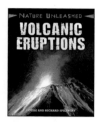

Volcanic Eruptions

Volcano Danger • Volcanoes in Action • Mount St. Helens • Pinatubo • El Chichón • Mount Vesuvius • Santa Maria • Nevado del Ruiz • Mount Pelee • Krakatau • Santorini • Mount Tambora • Where in the World? • Glossary • For More Information • Index

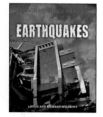

Earthquakes

Earthquake Danger • Earthquakes in Action • San Francisco, 1906 • Nepal, 2015 • Manjil-Rudbar, Iran, 1990 • Peru, 1970 • Kashmir, 2005 • Sichuan, 2008 • Japan, 1923 • Messina, Italy, 1908 • Tangshan, 1976 • Haiti ,2010 • Where in the World? • Glossary • For More Information • Index

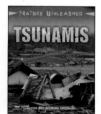

Tsunamis

Tsunami Danger • Tsunamis in Action • Flores Sea, Indonesia, 1992 • Chile, 1960 • Nankaido, Japan, 1946 • Tokaido, Japan 1923 • Papua New Guinea • San-Riku, Japan, 1933 • Andaman Sea-East Coast, 1941 • Moro Gulf, Philippines, 1976 • Japan, 2011 • Indian Ocean, 2004 • Where in the World? • Glossary • For More Information • Index

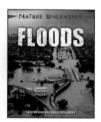

Floods

Flood Danger • Floods in Action • Mississippi Floods • Pakistan Floods, 2010 • Johnstown, 1889 • North Sea Floods, 1953 • North India Floods, 2013 • Vargas Tragedy, Venezuela, 1999 • Bangladesh, 1974 • Yangtse River Flood, 1998 • Ganges Delta, 1970 • Yellow River, China, 1931 • Where in the World? • Glossary • For More Information • Index

Hurricanes

Wind and Storm Danger • Tropical Storms in Action • Great Galveston Hurricane, 1900 • Typhoon Nina, 1975 • Hurricane Katrina, 2005 • Typhoon Bopha, 2012 • Hurricane Mitch, 1998 • Typhoon Tip, 1979 • Hurricane Camille, 1969 • Labor Day Hurricane, 1935 • Hurricane Patricia, 2015 • Typhoon Haiyan, 2013 • Where in the World? • Glossary • For More Information • Index

Wildfires

Fire Danger • Fires in Action • 2010 Russia • Ash Wednesday, 1983 • Landes Forest, 1949 • Black Saturday, 2009 • Miramichi, 1825 • Black Dragon, 1987 • Matheson Fire, 1916 • Cloquet Fire, 1918 • Peshtigo Fire, 1871 • Indonesia, 2015 • Where in the World? • Glossary • For More Information • Index